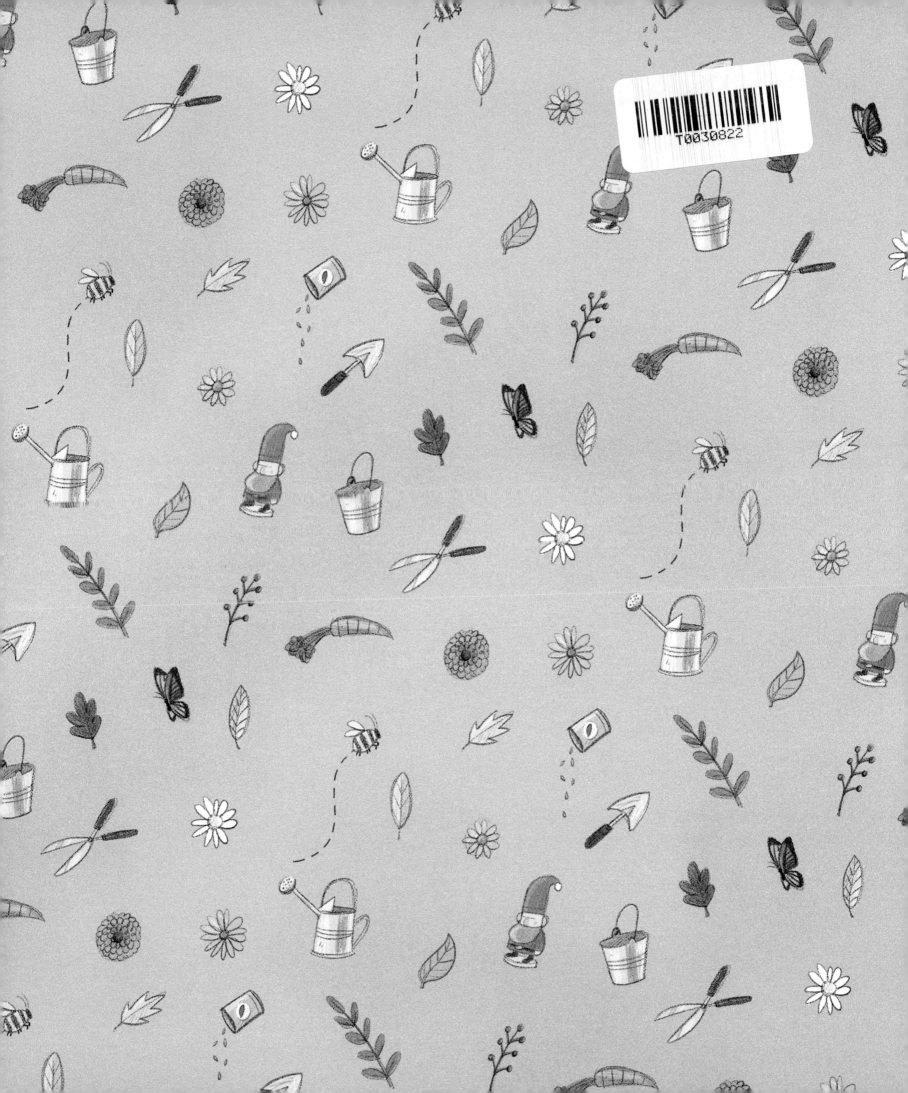

For Abby, Ginger, and Jen,
who make things grow
AW

Text copyright © 2022 by Allan Wolf
Illustrations copyright © 2022 by Daniel Duncan

First edition 2022

Library of Congress Catalog Card Number pending
ISBN 978-1-5362-0455-1

21 22 23 24 25 26 APS 10 9 8 7 6 5 4 3 2 1

Printed in Humen, Dongguan, China

This book was typeset in Clichee.
The illustrations were created digitally.

Candlewick Press
99 Dover Street
Somerville, Massachusetts 02144

www.candlewick.com

BEHOLD OUR MAGICAL GARDEN

Poems Fresh from a School Garden

Allan Wolf

illustrated by Daniel Duncan

CANDLEWICK PRESS

BEHOLD OUR MAGICAL GARDEN

In our garden, can you see?
A bird? A bug? A bumblebee?
A leaf? A breeze? A dogwood tree?
Behold our magical garden.

In our garden, what's in store?
A toolshed with a broken door?
A stray cat with a lion's roar?
Behold our magical garden.

In our garden, can you see?
An ear of corn? A pack of seeds?
A tepee made of greenery?
Behold our magical garden.

In our garden, can you spy?
A winding path where kids walk by?
A berry bush! A butterfly!
Behold our magical garden.

In our garden, can you see?
A compost bin? Some broccoli?
Rain barrels? Shovels? Pumpkins? Peas?
Behold our magical garden.

In our garden, can you find?
A bucket and a ball of twine?
A finger-painted welcome sign?
Behold our magical garden.

In our garden, can you see?
A grand adventure? And it's free!
A green delicious fantasy?
Behold our magical garden.

WELCOME

WE GROW IT FOR OURSELVES

We plotted out our garden
when the new school year began.
We were looking to the future.
We were dreaming of a plan.

Now the day has come for planting.
Now we've gathered up our seed.
Watch us writing lines of poetry
with furrows in the field.

Push a seed into the soil.
Push another by its side.
Turn the dirt into the hole.
Leave it be, and let it hide.

Watch the green reach up to drink the sun
a little more each day.
Pull the weeds out that surround it.
Give it water on the way.

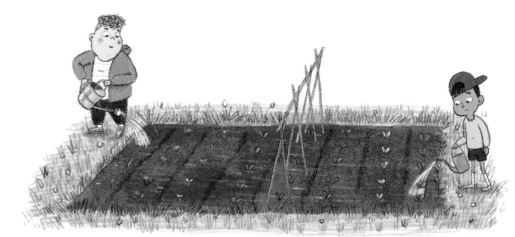

Come the harvest, we'll take baskets
and we'll stoop to pick the beans,
squash, peas, pumpkins, lettuce, peppers,
carrots, kale, and collard greens.

No supermarket mysteries.
No helpful garden elves.
We know our food is magic 'cause
we grow it for ourselves.

MAKING OBSERVATIONS

We are making observations.
We are writing what we see.
We are adding helpful sketches
of each plant's anatomy.

We write data in a notebook
on a shelf inside the shed.
Has the spinach started bolting?
Are the peppers turning red?

We are making observations.
We record the weather facts.
Is it sunny? Is it cloudy?
Is it raining dogs and cats?

We are keeping track of progress
in the garden day by day.
From the moment spring comes calling
until winter's here to stay.

GARDEN WONDERERS

I wonder. I wonder how an ant must feel
to be just a tiny ant and be a thing so small.
I wonder. I wonder if he looks at me,
and he wonders what it's like to be a kid so tall.

I wonder if ants have brothers and sisters.
I wonder if ants have uncles and aunts.
I wonder if ants have moms and dads
who make them go to school wearing six-legged pants.

I wonder. I wonder why a lightning bug can't thunder.
I wonder why a beetle doesn't have a drum to beat.
I wonder, Praying Mantis, are you praying for forgiveness
for the lightning bugs, the beetles, and the husbands that you eat?

I wonder, Little Sparrow, flying deadly as an arrow,
as you snatch the praying mantis, do you listen to her plea?
I wonder, Were I flea-sized, and these tiny creatures *me*-sized,
would the mantis, ant, the beetle, and the sparrow all eat *me*?

THE SECRET SEEDS

We seeds hold tomorrow
inside our shells.
What will we be?
We will not tell.
To find out what,
you'll have to wait
and watch us grow
from grain to great.

GERMINATION CELEBRATION

Like everything in life that grows,
all plants begin as embryos.
An embryo's an unborn sprout
who dreams a dream of getting out.
Inside her coat she sleeps and waits
until the day she finally breaks
the seed coat with a single root.
And new leaves quickly follow suit
and stretch out wide to celebrate.
And that's how all seeds germinate.

GREENHOUSE GUESSES

Five little sprouts in a greenhouse tray.
Dreaming of the plants they'll become one day.

The first little sprout, with a whimsical chant,
says, "Maybe I'm a sun-gold tomato plant!"

The second little sprout says, "Oh, my gosh!
Maybe I'm zucchini or an acorn squash."

The third little sprout says, "Maybe I'm a pea,
or a bean, or a carrot, or a broccoli."

The fourth little sprout thinks long and hard.
"Maybe I'm a spinach. Or a lettuce. Or a chard."

The fifth little sprout says, "What will *I* be?
Maybe I'm the world's tallest redwood tree
with an eagle's nest at the very tip-top,
and leaves of gold, and an ice cream shop!"

The moral is. No matter how small they seem,
even little sprouts can dream big dreams.

MARCH OF THE GARDEN VOLUNTEERS

Without warning, we appear.
We're the garden volunteers.

Rising from the compost bin,
volunteers are moving in.

Rising in between the rows,
volunteers are on the grow.

Cucumber and po-tay-TOE!
Volunteers are growing rogue.

Watermelon, to-may-TOE!
Where'd we come from? We don't know.

Pumpkin, squash, and zu-cchi-NI!
Volunteers are wild and free!

Over here and over there,
volunteers are everywhere.

Over there and over here,
we're the garden volunteers.

V-O (V-O)
L-U (L-U)
N-T (N-T)
E-E-R-S!
Garden volunteers!

Dill

Catnip

Thyme

Oregano

THE SECRET INGREDIENT

We are the flavors and the scents,
the mystery ingredients.
We make the secret sauce superb.
The one, the only . . . garden herbs!

We're *de rigueur*! We're all the rage.
Dill, oregano, and sage.
Parsley, basil, lemon balm.
Peppermint and tarragon.

Lavender for smelling pretty.
Catnip for a happy kitty.
Just a pinch! It won't take much
to give your food that final touch.

A dash of freshly chopped-up chives
will make your salad come alive.
To make your salsa taste sublime,
just add cilantro every thyme.

Smoothies, pizza sauce, or curry,
herbs add flavor in a hurry.
So listen to our sage advice:
plant herbs to give your garden spice!

Lemon Balm

Sage

Lavender

Mint

Basil

Tarragon

Chive

Parsley

LATIN NOMENCLATURE

Tomato. Okra. Eggplant. Spinach.
Popcorn, peas, and lettuce.
Our common names are so mundane
it's easy to forget us.

That's why Linnaeus gave us each
a scientific label.
And here's a few that you can use
while sitting at the table.

Say "Pass the *Pisum sativum*"
whenever you want peas.
Or *"Abelmoschus esculentus*
(that's the okra), please."
Solanum lycopersicum
is juicy and refreshing.
Solanum melongena might be, too
(but I'm just guessing).
Spinacia oleracea
is excellent in quiche.
And *Lactuca sativa*
puts the L in BLT.
And when you order popcorn
at the movies, you can utter
"I'd like my *Zea mays everta*
served with salt and butter."

All common plants have fancy names,
like everything in nature.
We're easy to identify
through Latin nomenclature!

DIARY OF A CARROT

DAY 1
I suddenly wake.
It is dark. I think
I am a baby chick
hatching from my shell.
Sleep.

DAY 3
I am *not* a baby chick.
I seem to have
a long white tail.
I think I am a mouse.
Sleep.

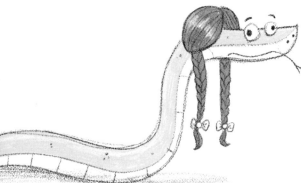

DAY 10
I am *not* a mouse.
I wiggle down
into the dirt. I think
I am a worm.

DAY 20
I am *not* a worm!
I am twice as long now.
Slender strands reach out. I think
I am a snake . . . with hair?

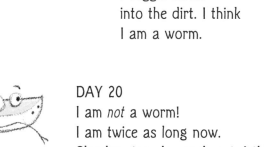

DAY 30
I am *not* a hairy snake.
But now long green blades
are reaching out from my head.
I think I am a helicopter. Hooray!

DAY 45
I am *not* a helicopter.
The green blades have multiplied.
They sprout from my head
like tentacles. I feel water all around.
I think I am an octopus.

DAY 60
I am *not* an octopus.
A rabbit nibbles on my hair! It tickles.
Hidden in the dirt,
my body grows thicker.
So much waiting.
I don't know what I am!

DAY 75
An exciting day.
I feel a yank at my hair.
I am raised in the air.
I am tossed in a basket
with others like me.
I think it is a birthday party!

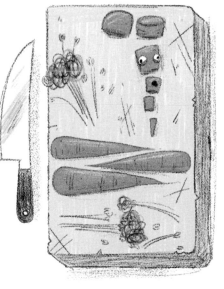

DAY 77
This is not a birthday party.
A human cuts off all my hair.
And chop-chop-chops me up.
I think I am dinner!

DAY 78
Spent all day in the dark.
Last thing I heard was
crunch, crunch, crunch.
Then, "Mmmmmm."

I think I was delicious.

THE THREE SISTERS

Poem for Three Vegetables

They call us the Three Sisters:
we're corn, bean, and squash.
Three flourishing sisters,
one nourishing meal.

Three ancient old sisters,
three histories braided
through stories of
Native American fields.

Three tangled-up sisters:
we can't tell exactly
where one plant begins
and another one ends.

They call us Three Sisters;
we're constant companions.
From planting to harvest,
inseparable friends.

THE GREEN BEAN BOWER

after William Carlos Williams

so much depends
upon

a green bean
bower

covered with vine
leaves

climbing the bamboo
poles

POTATO EXCAVATION SITE

In spring, just after final frost,
they planted us in mounded rows.
From every blind white eye we lost,
they hoped a dozen more would grow.

We've waited. Now the time is right.
Above we're brown and withered vines.
Below we're newborns sleeping tight,
our slender fingers intertwined.

Like garden archaeology,
they use their shovels carefully.
Russet? Purple? Yukon gold?
What treasures will our cradle hold?

A GARDEN RIDDLE FOR ALL SEASONS

In spring she wears a new green hat.
In summer she makes climbing fun.
In autumn she's a calico cat.
In winter she's a skeleton.
Who am I? And what is she?
I'm a kid! And she's a _____ !

POETREE

A treetop is a magic thing,
a home for wind and fur and wings.
A place where squirrels can make a nest.
A roost where weary birds can rest.
A home for wind and fur and wings,
a treetop is a magic thing.

Me trunk.
Me stand
up tall and
long. Me
rough. Me
tough. Me
very strong.
Me branch
out spring
and summer-
time, so you
can have a
place to climb.

The hide-away half of the tree
is the half of the tree you don't see.
The hide-away half underground
grows its roots without making a sound.
The hide-away half down below
spreads as wide as the top as it grows.
The hide-away half of the tree can be found
living all of its hide-away life upside down.

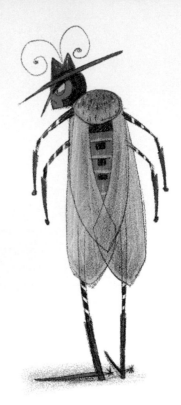

GOOD BUG, BAD BUG

or The Good, the Bad, and the Buggly

Your bountiful garden
is a free salad bar,
so be sure that you know
who your customers are.

We're bad bugs.
We're foragers.
Ravenous gatherers.
Plant-hungry hoarders,
we travel in packs.

We're good bugs,
lone hunters who
prey on the foragers.
Secretive, stealthy.
Ka-POW! Sneak attack!

We're bad bugs.
We're picky,
persnickety snackers,
and only particular
garden plants do.

We're good bugs.
We'll be there
whatever your species.
Tomato or turnip,
we'll watch over you.

Next time you see insects
abuzz in the garden,
think twice before
grabbing that swatter or spray.

It could be a good bug
who's come to the rescue,
in search of a snack
at the bad bug buffet.

WE ~~TREAT~~ YOUR FOOD LIKE IT'S OUR OWN

A Garden Pest Poem

Hornworm, grasshopper, snail, squash bug,
Japanese beetle, cutworm, slug.
Don't think of us as nasty pests;
consider us your garden guests.
Plant your garden. Let it grow.
And then leave town a month or so.
And while you're gone vacationing,
we'll stay and keep an eye on things.
We'll tend the crops. We'll work the soil.
We'll make sure nothing rots or spoils.
Perhaps we'll take a *tiny* taste,
but just so nothing goes to waste.
Relax and leave us here alone.
We'll treat your food like it's our own.

When you return and find just dirt,
we'll smile and ask,

What's for dessert?

SONG OF THE SONGBIRDS

From up above or down below
we watch the garden treasures grow.
We hop. We fly. We harmonize.
We add our voices to the show.

We rid the air of gnats and flies
and eat the bugs who otherwise
would feast on every plant they see.
We hunt. We feed. We fertilize.

We're blue jay, thrush, and towhee.
We are phoebe, wren, and chickadee.
Stately cardinal. Lowly crow.
Catbird in the dogwood tree.

Bluebird, blackbird, robin, sparrow,
chimney swift, and purple martin.
More than pretty songs with wings,
we're faithful garden guardians.

SONG OF THE FRIENDLY FLOWERS

Dainty ornamental flowers
blessed with secret superpowers.
Loyal garden crop protectors.
Bodyguards for garden bowers.

Peace projectors. Sun collectors.
Fertile pollen. Vital nectar.
Help the garden pollinate.
Honeybee and bloom connector.

Daisy sun. And hosta shade.
Delicate but not afraid.
Usefulness in beauty clad.
Fragrant, color-rich cascade.

Sunflowers make a garden glad.
Flying insect landing pads.
Bowing heavy seeded faces.
Gangly good Sir Galahads.

Need to brighten dreary spaces?
Try zinnias in flower vases.
Got the blues? Or caught a cold?
Chrysanthemum and echinacea.

Pesky rabbits getting bold?
Keep them out with marigold.
Calendula for youthful skin
in case your skin is getting old.

Cosmo and nasturtium.
Peony. Poppy. Black-eyed Susan.
More than pretty scented things,
we're faithful garden guardians.

What's even *more* incredible?
Some of us are edible!

ATTILA THE HEN AND THE MYSTICAL EGG PLANT

An Absolutely True Story That Never Happened

We had a pet chicken: Attila the Hen.
She lived twenty years and a day.
We thought she might live to one hundred, but then
our beloved old bird passed away.

We buried Attila out back by the beans,
and we murmured a few solemn words.
Then round in a ring, we all started to sing
"Kumbaya" to that wonderful bird.

The loss wasn't easy, but over the winter,
Time helped all our sorrow take flight.
And later that May on a magical day
we were met with a startling sight.

Where Attila had been there now stood a strange plant
with magnificent feather-like leaves.
It was bushy and round and made soft clucking sounds
when its branches would brush in the breeze.

We stood looking down at the plant we had found
when our teacher cried out in surprise
as we noticed some white shiny shapes catch the light:
perfect eggs of a miniature size!

Now when we eat breakfast, we think of Attila,
the chicken who free-ranged and rambled.
She left us a tree and a legacy we
can enjoy over easy or scrambled.

AN INTERVIEW WITH THE SUN

Who are you, sir, and what's your name?
Do you ever get tired of shining?
Do you ever grow weary of living in flame?
Is your hot endless fire declining?

    I am the sun. You know me well.
    My name is simply Sun.
    I don't grow tired that I can tell.
    My job is never done.

Where do you go? Do you have friends
who keep your furnace churning?
Or relatives who feed and tend
your flames to keep them burning?

    Each night I leave the place you are
    to shine upon some other land,
    each day returning from afar
    to shine upon your brother and

    your sister, and your cousins and
    your father and your mother and
    relations by the dozens. But
    for *me* there is no other and

    I am, alas, a lonely Sun.

You have no son or daughter?

    That's right. I am the only one.

Would you like a glass of water?

    I would indeed, dear friend. Thank you.
    I'm thirsty—there's no doubt.

Thus sadly ends this interview—
the water put him out!

THE BAD BREEZE

A morning breeze blew through our hair.
We felt as if someone was there
behind us, breathing on our shoulder.
Then the breeze, becoming bolder,
snatched our hats off as it blew.
I think that breeze was rude!

Me too!

THE SECRET OF THE CLOUDS

We saw up in the sky by chance
a rain cloud who had lost his pants.
But luckily he wore a pair
of silver lining thunder-wear.

WATER LINES
A Poem for Two Voices

Voice 1: Raindrops   Voice 2: Water

drip drop drip drop

                      water from the rain cloud

drip drop drip drop

                      water on the rooftop

drip drop drip drop

                      water down the downspout

drip drop drip drop

                      water in the rain barrel

drip drop drip drop
drip drop drip drop   water in the drip hose
drip drop drip drop   water in the water can
drip drop drip drop   water on the green plants
drip drop wet ground water on the wet ground

drip drop drip drop
Water all around!   Water all around!

(Read the *drip drop* lines softly, with the steady tick-tock rhythm of a clock or metronome. As shown, at first, voices 1 and 2 take turns speaking, then they speak at the same time. Divide the two voices among as many readers as you like.)

FOR BIG RED

Our garden ship
with dented metal hull,
rough cracked handles,
leaky, squeaky, threadbare tire.
Older than any one of us.
Holder of things
too heavy for our hands.
You are the helper.
You are the friend
who is always there
and never complains.

Even in the rain.

MYSTERY BY THE COMPOST BIN

A mystery feather
by the compost bin;
a black-and-yellow feather
by the compost bin;
a telltale feather
hidden by weeds,
next to some half-eaten
sunflower seeds.

THE FBI OF COMPOST

Break it all down.
Organic decomposers.
Break it all down.
Table scrap disposers.
Break it all down.
Composting composers.

Fungus
and Bacteria,
Invertebrates abound.

We're the FBI,
and we break it all down!

Fuzzy moldy Wonder bread?
Fungus in the bin.
Mushrooms in the flower bed?
Put 'em in the bin.

Fuzzy moldy Wonder bread.
Mushrooms all around.
The fungus is amongus
and we break it all down!

Billions of bacteria.
Billions in the bin.
Biomass hysteria.
Put 'em in the bin.

Tiny, near invisible.
An army indivisible.
Bacteria's responsible
for breaking it down!

Vigorous invertebrates
crawling in the bin.
We aerate and we separate.
Put 'em in the bin.

We're the bug and the slug
and the beetle. On our backs we
carry the bacteria like symbiotic taxis.
Worms turn the dirt
when they wiggle underground.

Invertebrates are vigorously
breaking it down.

Organic decomposers.
Break it all down.
Table scrap disposers.
Break it all down.
Composting composers.
Break it all down.

Fungus
    and Bacteria,
        Invertebrates abound.

We're the FBI,
and we break it all down!

POPCORN DUTY!

Today is popcorn duty!
It's our favorite garden job.
We shuck the husks by hand.
We pluck the kernels from the cob.

Our teacher pours the kernels
and he heats them in a pan.
And as the kernels start to pop,
we finally understand:

We sort of hate to say it,
but before corn-husking duty,
we always thought that popcorn
came in buckets from the movies!

SOMEONE TOOK THE GARDEN TOOLS

Someone took the garden tools
we keep inside the shed.
Someone took the garden tools
while we were home in bed.

Someone took the garden tools,
the only tools we had.
Someone took the garden tools.
Now all of us feel bad.

A lady with a microphone
conducted interviews.
"Someone took the garden tools!"
we told the evening news.

Next morning, when we went outside,
the whole class stopped to stare!
Our teacher wiped her eyes and cried
to see what waited there.

Spilling from the toolshed door
were shovels, hoes, and rakes,
buckets, clippers, pruning saws,
bailing twine, and stakes.

A dozen pairs of rubber boots.
A dozen pairs of gloves.
And a note that said, "To all of you.
From all of us. With love."

The sum of a community
is greater than its parts.
Someone took the garden tools
but could not take our hearts!

The tool that can't be taken
or replaced like all the rest.
Your most important garden tool
is beating in your chest.

OUTSIDE IN OUR WINTER GARDEN

Outside in our winter garden
springtime shouts
have withered to whispers.
Cardinals call from barren branches,
"Gardens come and go!"

Breezes rustle the straw-strewn plots,
the curled leaves, the brittle stalks,
the wrinkled leather of the lingering fruit:
afterthoughts in the compost bin.
"Gardens come and go!
Gardens come and go!"
Ruby-feathered valentines
in fresh white snow.

Snowflakes whiten dry brown vines
of tomatoes long eaten, or stepped on, or stewed.
Lazy clouds pause, heavy-flecked with fairy ice.
The stray cat meows loudly in search of scraps;
she exhales puffs of mist into the morning.
Ruby-feathered valentines
in fresh white snow.
Cardinals rest in barren branches.
"Gardens come and go!"

A lanky lone asparagus, gone to seed,
dreams she's a cattail dancing in the spring.

"Gardens come and go!
Gardens come and go!"
Cardinals nest in barren branches.
"Gardens come and go!"
Ruby-feathered valentines
in fresh white snow.
Cardinals sing from barren branches,
"Gardens come and go!"

AUTHOR'S NOTE

On my travels as a visiting author, I have seen hundreds of school gardens. Some are very simple, just flowers and vegetables growing in clay pots. Some are fancy "outdoor classrooms" with greenhouse nurseries, composting bins, winding walkways, and well-stocked toolsheds. Some schools even have a full-time garden teacher. Just remember, whether it is big or small, a school garden has big magic.

Among your most important garden tools are a notebook and a pen or pencil. Keep a journal of what you do and when you do it. Record your observations. Draw pictures of what you see. Use the poems in this book as a model and write your own.

The word *kindergarten* is made up of two German words: *Kinder* (child) and *Garten* (garden)—literally a place where children grow. The teacher is the gardener. The students are the crop! No matter what grade you are in, there is nothing more magical than growing things.

Plus a garden is the only classroom where you get to eat your schoolwork!

NOTES ON THE POEMS

BEHOLD OUR MAGICAL GARDEN
Each stanza in this poem has four lines. The first three lines rhyme. The fourth line is the same in every stanza. Try writing a poem of your own using rhyme and repetition.

WE GROW IT FOR OURSELVES & MAKING OBSERVATIONS
Look at these two poems side by side and read them both aloud. They share a similar rhythm and rhyme. Can you see other similarities? Can you see how they are different?

GARDEN WONDERERS
Try writing your own poem about something common that we usually take for granted. It can be a person, a place, or a thing. Ask your subject questions, and imagine what its secret life might be like.

THE SECRET SEEDS
This poem is written in first person plural, meaning it has more than one speaker—seeds. Look for other poems in this book that are written in first person plural. There are a lot!

GERMINATION CELEBRATION
This poem is made up of rhyming couplets (pairs of lines that rhyme). See if you can count them. And keep your eyes out for more rhyming couplets in other poems.

GREENHOUSE GUESSES
More rhyming couplets! If *you* could grow up to be a plant, what kind of plant would you be? The title of this poem is a play on words—a variation on the phrase "greenhouse gases."

MARCH OF THE GARDEN VOLUNTEERS
This poem is a botanical twist on a military chanting rhyme called a cadence call, sometimes referred to as a jody. Private Willie Lee Duckworth came up with the first cadence call, "Sound Off," in 1944. The steady rhythm of the words helps the soldiers stay in step. The call-and-response chanting keeps them breathing evenly. Try reading this poem out loud as you march in place. One reader should be the drill sergeant. The others should repeat each line.

THE SECRET INGREDIENT
Puns (words misused on purpose, suggesting other sound-alike words or meanings) should be in every poet's toolbox. The last two stanzas of this poem each contain a pun. Can you find them?

LATIN NOMENCLATURE
This poem works best if you read it out loud and pronounce the Latin words as shown. It may be difficult at first, but once you've memorized the Latin words, you can use them to impress your family and friends when you are eating.

DIARY OF A CARROT
Try writing your own diary poem from the point of view of any animal or object. What events would *you* find confusing as you experienced them for the first time?

THE THREE SISTERS
Try reading this poem out loud with two friends. Divide the lines into speaking parts.

THE GREEN BEAN BOWER

This is an "after poem" (a poem written in the style of or in response to another poet's poem). This poem is modeled directly after "The Red Wheelbarrow" by William Carlos Williams. Read the original and compare the two. Try writing your own version about some common object in your school garden.

POTATO EXCAVATION SITE

The first two stanzas of this poem have an ABAB CDCD rhyme scheme. That's a challenging writing task since the poet must think of two pairs of rhyming words for every stanza. In this example, the rhyming pattern changes in the last stanza. See if you can tell the difference.

A GARDEN RIDDLE FOR ALL SEASONS

Did you guess the answer? Try writing your own riddle poem. Remember to give your reader one final clue by ending the second-to-last line with a word that rhymes with the answer to your riddle.

POETREE

This is a shape poem (sometimes called a concrete poem): the text is laid out on the page in a way that illustrates the poem's topic. "Poetree" is really three shape poems in one. Can you identify all three?

BUGS ON STRIKE!

This protest poem is a simple rhyming couplet, so it is catchy and easy to memorize and can be repeated as a chant or call-and-response. Try writing your own two-line protest poem from the point of view of some common object (a tennis shoe, a trash can, a playground slide, or whatever you like).

GOOD BUG, BAD BUG

This poem can be read by a group of any size divided into three speaking parts: good bugs, bad bugs, and narrators. The poem's subtitle is a play on the classic western movie *The Good, the Bad, and the Ugly*.

WE TREAT YOUR FOOD LIKE IT'S OUR OWN

This poem is an example of irony, or sarcasm, because the speakers are saying one thing while meaning something completely different.

SONG OF THE SONGBIRDS & SONG OF THE FRIENDLY FLOWERS

These two poems share a special rhyming pattern made famous in Robert Frost's poem "Stopping By Woods on a Snowy Evening." In each stanza, the first, second, and fourth lines all rhyme with one another, while the third line rhymes with the first, second, and fourth lines of the next stanza. At a point, though, in each of these poems, this rhyming pattern is broken. Can you tell where?

ATTILA THE HEN AND THE MYSTICAL EGG PLANT

This poem is my own version of a cowboy poem. Like most cowboy poems, it has a romping rhythm and tells a long (and slightly goofy) story. Sometimes the rhyme is at the end of the line; sometimes the rhyme is in the middle.

AN INTERVIEW WITH THE SUN

This poem is fun to read as a team, with one person reading the part of the sun. One, two, or even more people can read the part of the reporter. By now you should notice the ABAB rhyming pattern.

THE BAD BREEZE & THE SECRET OF THE CLOUDS

Both these poems are good examples of personification, meaning they give human characteristics to nonhuman things.

WATER LINES

The *drip, drop* repetition in this poem is an example of onomatopoeia, words that sound like the thing they describe.

FOR BIG RED

This poem is an example of free verse, which doesn't follow a prescribed structure, rhythm, or rhyme pattern. And like "The Green Bean Bower," it is an "after poem"—also inspired by "The Red Wheelbarrow" by William Carlos Williams.

MYSTERY BY THE COMPOST BIN

This is what I call a snapshot poem. Think of it as a single frame from the middle of a movie or a photograph taken at a crime scene. Can you take the clues (the compost bin, the feather, and the half-eaten seeds) and turn them into a story with a beginning, a middle, and an end?

THE FBI OF COMPOST

This poem has rhythmical words that dance to a steady, obvious beat—perfect for a rap battle between three readers.

POPCORN DUTY!

This is my own version of a jump rope rhyme. Recite it as you jump rope. Or create your own hand gestures to go with the words.

SOMEONE TOOK THE GARDEN TOOLS

This poem is based on a real event that happened, twice, to a school garden just a couple blocks from my house!

OUTSIDE IN OUR WINTER GARDEN

This is another example of a free-verse poem. It has a plan of its own. It does not try to fit any prescribed pattern of rhyme or rhythm. Even so, it *does* boast a rhyme or two, and the repetition of some lines is very rhythmical. Can you find the rhymes and the repetition?

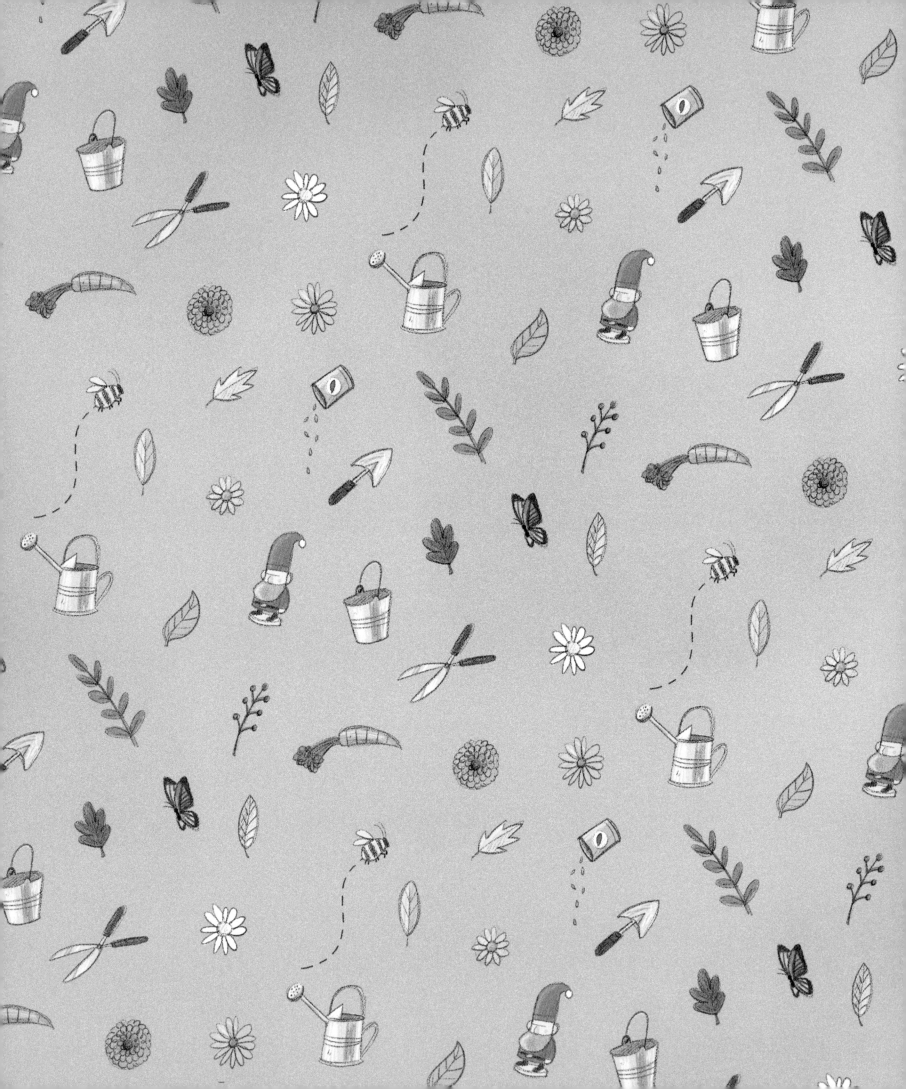